Mah-Jongg

D1502041

Mah-Jongg

Basic Rules & Strategies

Dieter Kohnen

Sterling Publishing Co., Inc.
New York

CONTENTS

We thank Hartung Games for permission to print the game tiles.

Photos: Achim Kalk, Kelkheim
Drawings: Dieter Köhnen, Mönchengladbach

Library of Congress Cataloging-in-Publication Data

Köhnen, Dieter
  [Mah-Jongg. English]
  Mah-jongg : basic rules & strategies / by Dieter Köhnen.
    p.   cm.
  Includes index.
  ISBN 0-8069-0752-5
  1. Mah jong   I. Title.
GV1299.M3K64 1998
795.3'4–dc21
                              98-21164
                              CIP

Translated by Annette Englander
Edited by Rodman P. Neumann

5   7   9   10   8   6   4

Published 1998 by Sterling Publishing Company, Inc.
387 Park Avenue South, New York, N.Y. 10016
Originally published and © 1996 by Falken Publishing
Company GmbH, Niedernhausen
under the title *Mah-Jongg: Regeln, Techniken, Übungen*
English translation © 1998 by Sterling Publishing Co., Inc.
Distributed in Canada by Sterling Publishing
ᶜ/ₒ Canadian Manda Group, One Atlantic Avenue, Suite 105
Toronto, Ontario, Canada M6K 3E7
Distributed in Great Britain and Europe by Cassell PLC
Wellington House, 125 Strand, London WC2R 0BB, England
Distributed in Australia by Capricorn Link (Australia) Pty Ltd.
P.O. Box 704, Windsor, NSW 2759,
Australia
Printing in Hong Kong
All rights reserved

Sterling ISBN 0-8069-0752-5

Getting into the Game

History of Mah-Jongg

The origin of Mah-Jongg dates back about 4000 years (Tang dynasty). It was at first a game of the Chinese ruling class. Whether the tile game began as a card game or playing cards developed from the use of tiles is unclear. Many of the terms used in Mah-Jongg relate to cards. Thus, one speaks of one's tiles as a "hand," even though they are not held but rather stand in a rack on the table.

The rules of this game of luck were long a guarded secret; only the mandarins—the aristocrats and officials —at the court of the Emperor knew them. The game became available to all classes only when China became a Republic in 1911.

In 1920, an American, Joseph Babcock, introduced Mah-Jongg to the United States, from where it began its enthusiatic acceptance that spread to Europe and the rest of the world. The ancient game was at first played outside China according to rules that differed from group to group as players thought the game would be improved by their introduction of changes. This quickly became very confusing, so Babcock put together in 1925 the first official set of rules, including a summary of the traditional Chinese rules, with the addition of new American ways to play. American Mah-Jongg was further standardized in 1937 with the founding of the National Mah Jongg League, which yearly changes the hands and rules to add to the enjoyment of the game. Rules and strategies for a so-called **mixed-hand** variation of **traditional** Mah-Jongg are presented here. The **Japanese** variation, which essentially codifies the pure traditional game, is contrasted to the mixed-hand game.

The name Mah-Jongg comes from Chinese (literally "flax/hemp" "sparrow"), referring to the sound of the plant's leaves clicking in the wind and the bird chattering, which the clicking tiles bring to mind.

Idea of the Game

Generally, Mah-Jongg is played with four persons, designated as East, South, West, and North. A **full game** consists of at least **16 hands** of play, falling within **four rounds**. The principle of the game is similar to the card game Rummy; however, game tiles are used instead of cards.

Combinations are created through the passing, discarding, and claiming of tiles, just as might be done with cards. The players try, for example, to collect several **sets** of tiles of the same kind (**pairs, triplets—called pung, or four—called kong**) or consecutive **sequences** of tiles (**chow**). When you have collected a certain hand, i.e., a prescribed combination, you can end the game—"make **Mah-Jongg**."

The Special Characteristics of Mah-Jongg

Many procedures seem at first unnecessarily complicated to the beginner. Special characteristics include the use and meaning of the four winds (or directions); East, South, West, North. Note that the customary Chinese listing is not the same as for the compass. Each player is assigned a wind. The first player (the dealer) is always East; to the right is South; across is West; and to East's left is North. The order of play is counterclockwise.

Because the winds are of great importance, the game is also called Pung Chow, the game of the winds, in some provinces of China.

The tiles are divided into categories: **honor** tiles, **suit** tiles, and **bonus** tiles—the **flowers** and **seasons**—that may affect scoring; they are always declared and a substitute drawn. To distribute the tiles, unlike a card game where you would draw from a pile, in Mah-Jongg you draw them from a **wall**, which is built before play begins. The tiles are placed face down on the table and thoroughly mixed. Each player then draws tiles to build a wall in front of his rack; 36 tiles in 18 **stacks**—a stack is two tiles, one on top of the other.

The Goal of the Game

The goal of the game is to make Mah-Jongg (go out) by completing a hand. The object is to create a high-scoring complete hand quickly, consisting of four sets plus a pair, in order to win the hand.

There are many variations in scoring. Generally, scoring is a three-step process involving points, doubles, and payment. When a hand is won, the winner displays his hand and scores it. A maximum score of 500 points is often set, with a hand being called a **limit hand** that automatically receives the limit without calculation. A system of paying the winner is then used to settle the hand. The game lasts four rounds of at least four hands each.

The Rules in Brief

A Mah-Jongg game consists of four rounds, each round, in turn, of at least four games. Each round is named after a wind. The first is the East wind round, then follow South, West, and North wind rounds. The number of games that make up a round depends on whether the dealer wins his own deal (more about this on page 20). The tiles are arranged into stacks to build a wall and begin distribution. Once the tiles are distributed, the object of each game is for the players to try to form —with their tiles and those they draw anew from the wall or take from another's discard—certain combinations which count as many points as possible, and maybe to make Mah-Jongg (i.e., end the game).

One after another, each player takes one tile and discards one face up while naming it.

Hidden tiles may be taken from the wall, or—sometimes even when it is not your turn—you may declare and pick up the *last* tile discarded.

You are only allowed to pick up the discard if you are faster than another player, and if with it you can complete a combination. You must then meld (lay face up on your right) this combination; it counts less than a concealed combination which you collect by drawing from the wall. Accordingly, the combinations are called either concealed or melded.

The combinations consist of sets of three or four tiles or a pair. A set can be a sequence of three consecutive numbers of the same suit or a collection of three or four of the same kind—identical tiles.

Most of the combinations have Chinese names, which are announced aloud during the game. They are:

- **Chow** for a sequence,   `1`
- **Pung** for a set of three,   `2`
- **Kong** for a set of four,   `3`
- **Pair** for two of a kind.   `4`

When you need only one tile to complete your hand, your hand is said to be *ready*. It may be possible for you to make Mah-Jongg (to go out and end the game).

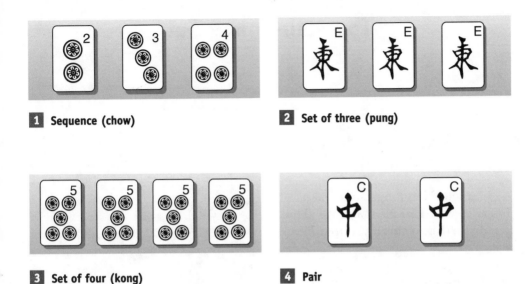

1 Sequence (chow)

2 Set of three (pung)

3 Set of four (kong)

4 Pair

A complete hand must contain four sets and a pair. The four sets may be sequences (chows) and three or four of a kind (pungs and kongs)—melded or concealed. The only thing is that no individual tile and (except in some game variations) no other pair may be included.

The values used in scoring can vary from group to group. Generally when the hand is finished, the points, which all the players have accumulated, are calculated. The points are multiplied by any applicable doubles, and then payment is made.

The person who has ended the game determines his points first, and receives a bonus for the Mah-Jongg. After that, the other players calculate their combinations.

The winner of that hand is the player who has made Mah-Jongg. It is possible that the player who Mah-Jongged might not have achieved the greatest number of points; then there is a "second" winner. The deal passes to the right, unless the dealer (East) has won, in which case East deals again. The round is complete when each of the four players has held and lost the deal. One complete game consists of four rounds, each named for the prevailing wind; East round first, then South round, West round, and North round fourth. Each player deals once (or more than once if he wins) in each round.

A complete game (at least sixteen hands) can last from one and a half to three or more hours.

The Mah-Jongg Set

Tiles

A complete Mah-Jongg set consists of 144 tiles with various markings. They are divided into three groups. There are:

♦ **108 suit tiles.** These are tiles on which balls, Chinese characters, and bamboo sticks are pictured .
♦ **28 honor tiles.** These are subdivided into **winds** and **dragons**, which in most game-sets are portrayed with Chinese characters. These may also have English letters in some sets.
♦ **8 bonus tiles.** These are subdivided into 4 **flowers** and 4 **seasons**, which are frequently characterized by respective picture portrayals, numbered 1 to 4 in two different colors.

Suit Tiles

These are the most plentiful tiles, and since there are four of each number in each suit, the desired combinations can be formed relatively easily with them. But in return, they also count less than combinations with the rarer honor tiles.

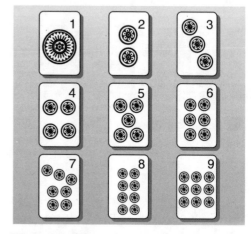

5 Balls (also called dots or circles)

The three suits are:

Balls (dots, circles),   **5**
Bamboos (sticks, bams, boos),   **6**
Characters (characks, cracks, wan).   **7**

Amongst themselves, they are of equal value, and they are comparable with the suits spades, clubs, hearts, and diamonds in card games.

Within each suit, they are counted from 1 to 9, symbolized by the respective number of circles or bamboo sticks, or the respective Chinese number. The first bamboo tile is often an

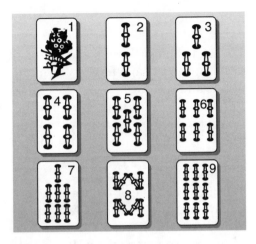

6 Bamboos (also called sticks, bams or boos)

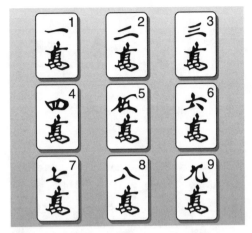

7 Characters (also called characks, cracks, or wan)

exception, being symbolized by a bird, the sparrow. The number 1 and number 9 tiles are called **terminals**. They are more valuable than the **simples**, 2s through 8s. Each of the nine tiles of a suit occurs four times. That means, there are three suits of 36 tiles each: overall 108 suit tiles.

8 Honor tiles: the dragons: white, red, and green

Honor Tiles

There are four tiles each of three different dragons and the four winds.

The three dragons may appear as red, green, or white dragons. Traditionally they are marked with Chinese characters, as well as by the letters B (or P), C, and F. **8**

These letters come from the Chinese names for these tiles. The red has the Chinese character Cheung—meaning center of the four directions—thus the letter "C." The green dragon has the Chinese character, Fa Choy—meaning "begin good luck"— thus the letter F. The white dragon is also called the bak board (or pak board)—thus the letter B (or P) within a rectangle.

Each of the three dragons exists four times, i.e., there are 12 dragon tiles overall.

The honor tiles are valued higher than the suit tiles because they are more rare.

9 Honor tiles: the four winds

10 Bonus tiles: the flowers

11 Bonus tiles: the seasons

The four winds—East, South, West, North—also occur four times each. They are imprinted with the corresponding Chinese characters as well as the English letters E, N, S, and W. **9**

In each hand, each player is assigned a wind. Each round is also known by the prevailing wind for that round. During its respective round each wind is important in scoring. A combination with the player's wind, or the round wind, has scoring advantages. (More about this on page 25.)

Bonus Tiles

The bonus tiles (flowers and seasons) differ in their characteristics from the honor and suit tiles. **10** **11**

The bonus tiles have a high value; they add points to the score, and when the wind associated with each is the prevailing wind, they can provide doubles to the total count.

If a player is dealt or draws such a tile, he melds it (places it face up on his right) and draws a substitute tile from the end-part of the wall, which is called "dead" wall. (More about the dead wall on page 15.)

Keep in Mind

Each of the bonus tiles is marked with a number that corresponds to a wind. That means that a player who has a bonus tile of his own prevailing wind gets more points.

The allocation is as follows: Flower or season tiles with a 1 belong to the East, with a 2 to the South, with a 3 to the West, and with a 4 to the North.

Additional Game Material

Many Mah-Jongg sets in addition to the 144 tiles also contain:

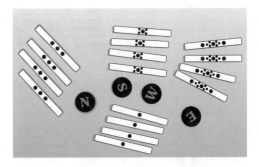

12 **Dics of the four winds and bones (also called counters)**

◆ Four discs imprinted with the winds—E, S, W, N. 12

There are usually three dice, which are used in conjunction with the discs to allocate one of the winds to each player. Each player throws a pair of dice and the highest roll becomes the East wind.

All three dice are sometimes used to determine the starting point in the wall for each deal.

◆ 72 bones, or counters—little calculation sticks with dots printed on them in different quantities. They are distributed evenly to all players. 12

The players can agree beforehand on the values of the bones. But the following allotments have proven to be useful:

10, 50, 100, and 500 points, or 10, 100, 500, and 1000 points.

When bones are not available, poker chips in different colors can be used.

◆ Some sets include racks. The racks have two functions. They are used to build the wall, and the tiles of one's hand can be set up in them.

First Quiz

1 How many tiles overall belong to the Mah-Jongg game?

2 How many tiles of the character suit does the game have?

3 How many tiles result from adding all of the bamboo, dragon, and flower tiles?

4 For which tiles are there only one each?

5 To which wind does the season tile 3 belongs?

6 Name the tiles, which belong to the suit tiles and those which belong to the honor tiles.

Answers: Page 46

Game Preparation

Seating Arrangement

There are many ways to determine who sits where and who will deal first. A simple way is for the players to seat themselves arbitrarily and each roll the dice. The player with the highest roll becomes the East wind and will deal.

There are more involved ways to determine seating, taking into account various superstitions. The players may agree to any procedure, such as the simple drawing of face-down discs or wind tiles. The seating order and play is counterclockwise, with South to the right of East, West across from East, and North to the left of East. The deal also passes to the right after East has lost the deal.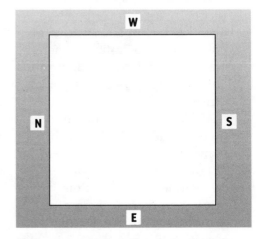

Seating arrangement—the first player (the dealer) is always East

One traditional way to determine seating is for the oldest player to mix the discs or wind tiles and arrange them face down, in a straight row. The person to his right now determines whether the outside left or the outside right tile or disc is the head of the row.

The next person to the right now must throw two dice. According to the total number of the pips, this player counts all participants counterclockwise, beginning with himself. The place where the last player counted is becomes East.

14

This player then throws the two dice again and counts counterclockwise once more.

The last counted player then takes the head tile or disc of the row, which was previously decided; the person to his right takes the second; the next to the right the third; and the last player the fourth.

Each player now has a tile or disc with one of the winds on it.

The person who has drawn East becomes the dealer and sits down at the place which was previously designated East. The others take their seats according to their wind, as shown in the picture.

The East wind prevails for the first round. After all four players have held and lost the deal, the second, or South, round follows, in which the South wind prevails, meaning that the player holding the South position assumes the role of East. In the third round, West prevails; and in the fourth, North.

Building the Wall

Out of the 144 suit, honor, and bonus tiles, the players build a "courtyard" wall. To do that, four sidewalls are formed, one by each player. The tiles are first mixed face down. Each player arranges 18 **stacks** (two tiles, one on top of the other) in a row. Each sidewall consists of 36 tiles. The walls are pushed together to form a square. The completed wall belongs to all the players. **14**

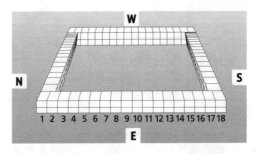

14 Closed wall with seating arrangement

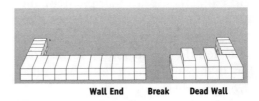

15 Breaking the wall

Breaking the Wall

To distribute tiles, the wall is broken. East as dealer takes on this task. **15**

Which side to break is sometimes decided by using a roll of the dice to count counterclockwise from the dealer. The dice may also be used to count stacks from the right to find the place to break the wall. A slightly simpler method is explained here.

East counts from the right seven stacks along his side of the wall and breaks through by removing the seventh pair.

East places those two tiles, the so-called **loose tiles**, individually to the right of the break—the lower tile onto the third and the upper onto the

16 The tiles of one player. To have a playing hand, he must declare the flower tile 3, placing it face up to his right, and draw a supplement tile.

fifth tile. These are **supplement** tiles that are taken to replace bonus tiles.

This portion of the wall to the right is called the "**dead wall**." No tiles other than supplement tiles are taken from the dead wall.

The Deal

East takes the first two stacks for himself. The next two stacks he gives to South, the next to West, and the next ones to North.

East repeats this distribution two more times so that each player has six stacks (12 tiles). East then draws two more tiles and distributes only one more tile to South, West, and then North. East has a hand of 14, whereas the other players have hands of 13.

Eeveryone waits to arrange his tiles until after the deal is complete. Each places them in such a way that the opponents cannot see them, standing in a row or set in a rack.

If any player has bonus tiles (flowers or seasons), he declares so right away by placing them face up in front of himself, and he draws a **supplement** tile from the dead wall for each. If any player draws a bonus tile again, he takes another supplement tile from the dead wall. **16**

Each player examines his tiles for possible combinations. Each is looking for elements from which sets can be built; sequences (chows), three of a kind (pungs), or four of a kind (kongs). A player may or may not arrange his hand; doing so or not is a matter of strategy.

Second Quiz

1 Which is correct?

A The seating arrangement is determined with the dice.

B The dice are used to determine which player's turn it is.

C With the dice, the player sequence is determined.

2 What is the sequence of the seating arrangement, beginning with the dealer?

3 What is the part of the wall on the right of the break called? And from which part of the wall are the tiles dealt?

4 How many tiles does each of the players get at the beginning of the game?

Answers: Page 46

Playing

Basic Playing Pattern

Mah-Jongg is played counterclockwise. The play begins at East, then ordinarily follows to South, West, and then North. One after another, the players take a tile and then discard one face up inside the wall in front of them. Each player's discards are kept apart from the others', and placed in order, from left to right.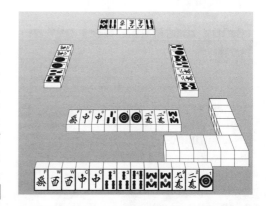

Since East is the dealer, he has one extra tile at the start. Play begins by East discarding a tile. It is the custom for each player to name aloud his discard. The player, whose turn it is, can choose between two possibilities:

◆ either he draws a concealed tile from the wall, or
◆ he picks up the last discarded tile after declaring the Chinese name of the set it will complete (chow, pung, kong)—and if he is faster than another player who can, out of turn, declare the last discard to make a set of three or four (pung or kong, only).

A player may only claim a discard at the time it is discarded. Any discard not picked up is then "dead."

17 Each player's discards are kept separate, placed face up inside the wall in front of him, in order from left to right.

If a player decides to draw a tile from the wall, he draws the next tile from the left end of the wall. If there is a stack—two tiles one on top of the other—he takes the upper tile.

When a player calls out for the discarded tile, he must declare the set that it completes. If it is the player's turn, then he can declare "chow" for a sequence, "pung" for three of a kind, and "kong" for four. If it is not the player's turn, he can only declare a pung or kong. When a set is formed with a discard, it must be melded—placed face up, to the right, in front of the player

If the declared set is a kong (four of a kind), melding the triplet you already have, adding the claimed tile, and then discarding will leave your hand missing a tile—you'll have 12 instead of 13. So a supplement tile is drawn from the dead wall. Only then do you discard.

Taking Discarded Tiles out of Turn

A player whose turn it is not may declare a pung or kong, claiming the discarded tile, and thus turn the game to his advantage—provided that:

◆ the declared combination can be completed and melded, and
◆ the player, who wants to declare out of turn, is clearly faster than the person whose turn it is.

Keep in Mind

Independent of the regular counter-clockwise sequence, play continues to your right if you have just successfully declared "pung" or "kong," skipping anyone between you and the player who discarded the tile you claimed. Play may not proceed to the right if it is again interrupted by another player declaring "pung" or "kong" and claiming your discarded tile.

The player whose turn it is can therefore prevent another player from declaring by quickly drawing from the wall or by himself declaring and claiming the discarded tile. If several players declare at the same time, the order of precedence is: pung (three of a kind) has precedence over chow (three in a sequence); kong (four of a kind) has precedence over pung or chow; and "Mah-Jongg," or going out, has the highest preference. If two players declare the same thing, the person, whose turn is next, gets the tile.

"Chow" may only be declared by the person whose turn it is.

Ending the Hand

Generally, a hand ends with a player making Mah-Jongg—going out.

To do that, the respective player either draws another tile from the wall, or he claims the last discarded tile to complete his hand and go out. He declares "Mah-Jongg."

In rare cases it can happen that several players declare "Mah-Jongg" for the same tile. Again, that person whose turn it is next takes precedence.

After Mah-Jongg is declared, the player's hand must be melded openly at once. **18**

If a player makes Mah-Jongg, the points of all the players are now scored. (For that, see page 25, "Settlement of a Hand.")

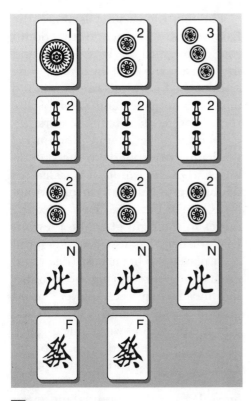

18 Melding the hand

The hand ends in a draw if no one has gone out by the time the wall is exhausted. If no player succeeds in making Mah-Jongg, then the hand stops, there is no settlement, and the deal passes to the right and a new hand begins.

Third Quiz

1 Which tile, or tiles, is a player whose turn it is allowed to take?
A Any tile inside the wall.
B The tile which was last discarded inside the wall.
C A tile from the wall.
2 Do the tiles lie concealed or face up in the courtyard, and are they all in the middle?
3 How many tiles must the player discard for one tile taken?
4 When must a combination be melded (laid out face up)?
A When a concealed wall tile completes the combination.
B When a discarded tile completes the combination.
C When it can be formed immediately after the deal.
5 How can a player, whose turn it is not, turn the game to his advantage and thus overleap the other players?
6 Which combination can you declare with the call "chow," which with "pung," and which with "kong"?
7 Which is the correct order of precedence:
A Mah-Jongg
Kong
Chow
Pung

(Continued next page)

B Mah-Jongg
    Pung
    Kong
    Chow
C Mah-Jongg
    Kong
    Pung
    Chow
D Mah-Jongg
    Chow
    Kong
    Pung

Answers: Page 46

The Course of the Game after the First Hand

At the end of the first hand, if it is not a draw, the score is calculated and the hand is settled. The deal then passes to the right, unless East (the dealer) has won. When East wins then there is a dealer's extra hand. East keeps the deal until there is a draw or he loses. There is no limit to the number of extra hands the dealer may play. These dealer's extra hands are in addition to the sixteen hands of the game.

When the deal passes to the right, the new dealer assumes the name East, and the other players take the names of the other winds in their usual counterclockwise order.

A round is complete when all four players have held and lost the deal—a minimum of four hands.

The first wind round is always the East round, the second the South round, the third the West round, and the fourth the North round. The discs of the four winds can be used to indicate the **prevailing wind** of the round and to identify the players.

When a player's wind position for the hand corresponds to the prevailing wind of the round, it is called his **double wind**, and has scoring advantages. Since the title "East" (dealer) moves to the right after the previous East (dealer) has lost a hand—until each player has been East (dealt and lost a hand) once during the round—this means that each player's wind postion for the hand will coincide with the prevailing wind at least once during play of a hand in each round. Thus, in the East round, each player will assume the title "East" at least once. During the South round, each will assume the title "South" at least once; during the West round, each will be "West" at least once, and so on for the North round.

It is not necessary for the players to change their seats; it is simply the wind directions that move to the right with each hand lost by the dealer—four times each round. The changing of the prevailing wind for each round is simply a way to designate the position of the double wind, so that each player has a scoring advantage at least once each round in a consistent manner.

The Combinations

The object of the game, as introduced earlier, is to "Mah-Jongg"—go out—by completing a hand composed of four sets of three or four tiles each, plus a pair. Each player collects the elements of these sets to form sequences, triplets, and sets of four.

Keep the Chinese names of these combinations in mind, since you need them to call out the tiles!

Chow (A Sequence)

Three consecutive tiles of the same suit—balls, bamboos, characters—is the combination called a sequence. *Chow* is the Chinese term for a sequence. A chow may only be declared for a tile discarded on the player's left. It does not matter with which number a sequence begins. **19**

You are not allowed to add a fourth tile to a sequence!

19 Chow: character suit sequence

20 Pung: white dragon triplet

Value of the Chow

With perhaps one exception (see "Premium Points for Mah-Jongg," page 27), chows have no score value and are used merely to complete a hand.

Pung (Triplet)

Three honor or suit tiles which are exactly the same— for example, three bamboo 4 tiles; three ball 1 tiles; three white dragon tiles—comprise a triplet. *Pung* is the Chinese term for a triplet. **20**

There are **exposed** and **concealed** pungs:

◆ Exposed are those in which the third tile was claimed from any other player's discard rather than drawn from the wall.

The exposed pung must be melded face up, to the right, in front of the player.

◆ Concealed pungs are obtained when a player having a pair of like tiles in his playing hand draws a third similar tile from the wall. The player does not have to declare this pung, but rather can choose to keep it concealed in his hand.

An exposed pung can be converted into a set of four (kong) only by the player's drawing a concealed tile from the wall that matches the other three. The player adds this fourth tile to the already melded pung. He must draw a supplement tile from the dead wall, before he discards a tile, in order to still have 13 tiles in his hand.

Value of the Pung

Pungs composed of honor tiles (dragons or winds) or of so-called terminal tiles (the numbers 1 and 9 of suit tiles) score 4 points exposed, and 8 points concealed.

Pungs composed of suit tiles with the numbers 2 to 8 score 2 points exposed, and 4 points concealed.

Kong (A Set of Four)

Four honor or suit tiles which are exactly the same—for example, four South wind tiles—comprise a set of four. *Kong* is the Chinese term for a set of four. **21**

21 Exposed honors kong: four south winds

22 Declared concealed bamboo kong: many prefer a convention of placing the two inside tiles face up and the two outside, face down.

Kongs can be formed in three ways:

◆ from a concealed pung in your hand and a discarded tile,
◆ from a concealed pung in your hand and a tile drawn from the wall,
◆ from a melded pung and a tile drawn from the wall.

Kongs also fall into three categories—**exposed, concealed,** or **declared concealed**:

◆ The exposed kong can be formed from a concealed pung and a discarded tile or a melded pung and a tile drawn from the wall. The exposed kong must be melded.

- A concealed kong is any four of a kind held in the hand—not declared and not melded. The concealed kong can only be formed from four dealt tiles or a concealed pung and a concealed tile drawn from the wall.
- A declared concealed kong is simply any concealed kong that the player choses to declare, and thus meld before Mah-Jongg is announced. A concealed kong can only be declared when it is your turn. A declared concealed kong is distinguished from the exposed kongs by melding it with two tile face down and two tiles face up. **22**

It is not necessary to declare a kong the moment it is made. A drawn tile that could be added to a melded pung or to a concealed pung in your hand may be kept and utilized for another combination; perhaps to form a chow or a pair. The advantage of a concealed kong is that the other players cannot recognize so easily what you collect. But for that reason, a concealed kong that has not been revealed until the player declares Mah-Jongg counts less—only as a pung—than either the exposed kong or declard concealed kong.

When a kong is declared and melded, you must take a supplement tile form the dead wall, before you discard. In case of a concealed kong, on the other hand, you do not get a supplement tile.

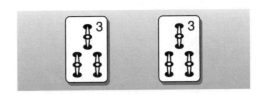

23 Bamboo pair

Value of the Kong

Kongs of honor and terminal suit tiles are worth 32 points when concealed but declared , 16 points exposed, and 8 points concealed.

Kongs of suit tiles of the numbers 2 to 8 score 16 points when concealed but declared, 8 points exposed, and 4 points concealed.

A Pair

To make Mah-Jongg you need to have a pair. Your hand may not contain more than this one pair (except in certain special hands)! **23**

A pair cannot be melded and then added to later to form a pung.

Value of a Pair

For most pairs—suit tiles and ordinary winds—there are no points. But a pair of dragons, a pair of the prevailing wind, or a pair of your own wind gets 2 points. When your own wind is the prevailing wind—a double wind—then the double wind pair gets 4 points.

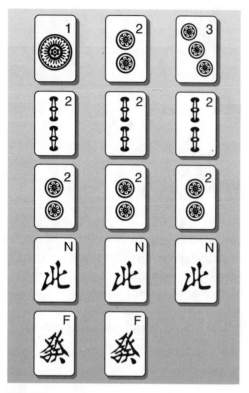

24 A completed hand without a season or flower tile

Completing a Hand

To make Mah-Jongg, you need a complete hand—four sets and a pair. It is largely arbitrary which sets are contained in it; only the end pair is obligatory.

A complete hand generally requires 14 tiles. But since you play with only 13 tiles, the player making Mah-Jongg does not discard. **24 25**

But a hand can also consist of more than 14 tiles—up to 18, when a player has four kongs and the end pair.

Chows are easiest; declared, concealed kongs are the hardest.

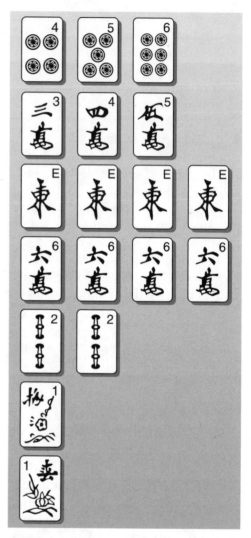

25 A completed hand with a season and flower tile

Collecting simple sets has the advantage that you can make Mah-Jongg more easily. But it is then possible for an opponent to score higher, winning once the hand is settled.

Special hands are the greatest challenge (see pages 48 to 59) but are also scored extraordinarily high.

Settling a Hand

Scoring Procedure

In the **traditional** game, only the winner scores points. But there are many variations in scoring, so it is best for the players to agree on how they will score before the first hand begins.

In the so-called **mixed-hand** game, all four players exchange points at the end of each hand. This difference in scoring has a profound effect on the character of play. The mixed-hand game tends not to be as fast, since each player is trying to collect high-scoring sets rather than trying to prepare his own hand to go out as soon as possible. Since the traditional scoring is straightforward, mixed-hand scoring is explained.

When a hand is won, the Mah-Jongg caller scores his hand first. To score his own hand, each player first sorts out the tiles that do not bring any points. Exposed sets are then scored, followed by declared, concealed ones.

Each player scores his points, applies any doubles, and rounds to the nearest 10 (because the lowest denomination of the bones or chips is 10). The highest final score is paid by the losing players with their bones.

The dealer (East) must always pay double or be paid double. In most playing circles, for the mixed-hand game, the losing players also settle points with each other by subtracting, for each pair of losers, the lower score from higher to arrive at their net score. The losing players settle their differences by exchanging bones—the difference going to the player with the higher score. If two losing players' scores are identical, then no payment is made. If East is a loser, he pays double the amount in settling with the others.

The winner is the only one who does not have to pay anything.

Example

If South calculates a final score of 20 points and West has 50, South must pay 30 points to West (50–20 = 30 net, paid to higher scorer, West).

Only after all of the players have scored their points, multiplied any applicable doubles, and rounded the total is it clear which player has won—that is, has the highest final score according to points—and whether it is the same player who has made Mah-Jongg.

Reaching Settlement

Especially while you are still new to playing a hand of Mah-Jongg, you should have readily at hand for each player's reference the "Point Table for Combinations," the "Premium Points for Mah-Jongg," the "Doubling Table," and the "Overview of Doubling" (on page 27).

That way, during the game, everyone can make reference to these tables to assist them in deciding on the best strategy.

Point Table for Combinations			
	exposed	concealed	declared concealed
Chow	-	-	-
Pair, consisting of own winds	-	2	-
Pair, consisting of prevailing winds	-	2	-
Pair, consisting of dragons	-	2	-
Pung, consisting of the numbers 2 to 8	2	4	-
Pung, consisting of the numbers 1 or 9	4	8	-
Pung, consisting of winds	4	8	-
Pung, consisting of dragons	4	8	-
Kong, consisting of numbers 2 to 8	8	4	16
Kong, consisting of numbers 1 or 9	16	8	32
Kong, consisting of winds	16	8	32
Kong, consisting of dragons	16	8	32
Flower or season tile	4	-	-

Premium Points for Mah-Jongg

Mah-Jongg call (going out)	20 points
Mah-Jongg out of the hand	20 points
Only chows and end pair, all of one suit	20 points
Only one suit, but no 1 or 9 (terminals)	20 points
Four pungs and a pair	2 points
Last tile self-drawn from the wall	2 points
Last tile as the very last tile from the wall	4 points
Last tile from the dead wall	4 points
Last tile completes the end pair	3 points
Last tile completes chow as center tile	2 points
End pair of winds or dragons	2 points
End pair of own wind	4 points
End pair of prevailing (round) wind	4 points

Doubling Table

Pung of dragons	double 1 x
Pung of winds	double 1 x
Pung of own wind	double 2 x
Pung of prevailing (round wind)	double 2 x
Pung of double wind (own wind is prevailing)	double 3 x
Each kong	double 1 x
Kong of winds	double 2 x
Kong of dragons	double 2 x
Kong own wind	double 3 x
Kong of prevailing (round) wind	double 3 x
Kong of double wind (own wind is prevailing)	double 4 x
Hand only one suit of dragons and winds	double 2 x
Hand only made of tiles of one suit	double 3 x
Hand only made of dragons	double 4 x
Hand only made of winds	double 4 x
Hand of terminal tiles 1	double 4 x
Hand of terminal tiles 9	double 4 x
Flower or season tiles of own wind	double 1 x
Four flower or four season tiles	double 2 x
All flower and all season tiles	double 5 x

Overview of Doubling		
1 x	multiply by	2
2 x		4
3 x		8
4 x		16
5 x		32
6 x		64
7 x		128
8 x	doubling: multiply by	256
9 x		512
10 x		1 024
11 x		2 048
12 x		4 096
13 x		8 192
14 x		16,384
15 x		32,768
16 x		65,536
17 x		131,072
18 x		262,144
19 x		524,288
20 x		1,048,576

Playing for Money

If all of the players agree to play for money, then you should set the values of the bones or chips at a very low amount. You should also determine an upper **limit** score for each hand, maximally between 500 and 1000 points. Very high point scores can easily come about in Mah-Jongg through doublings. In the absence of a point limit, it is even possible to exceed a score of a million points, as the following example shows. 26

Example

West has made Mah-Jongg in an East wind round and has self-drawn his last tile from the wall with which he completed the end pair. This is what the settlement looks like:

Mah-Jongg (going out)	20 points
4 flowers, 4 points each	16 points
4 seasons, 4 points each	16 points
Declared, concealed kong of white dragons	32 points
Declared, concealed kong of East winds	32 points
Declared, concealed kong of green dragons	32 points
Declared, concealed kong of South winds	32 points
Pair of West winds	2 points
Last tile self-drawn from the wall	2 points
Last tile completes the end pair	2 points
	186 points

This point total is now doubled:

All flower and all season tiles:	double 5 x
2 dragon kongs being doubled 2 x each:	double 4 x
South wind kong:	double 2 x
East wind kong (the prevailing wind):	double 3 x
hand made of only honor tiles:	double 4 x
	double 18 x

The 186-point total is doubled 18 times (2^{18}):

◆ 186 x 262,144 = 48,757,784. (rounded) = 48,757,780

That is the final point score, which West receives from North and from South; East, however, as the dealer, must pay double this number of points, i.e., 97,517,560. Thus, West receives overall 195,035,120 points!

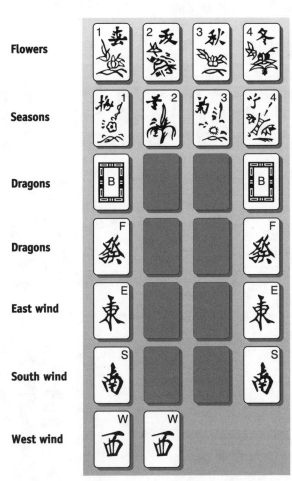

Flowers

Seasons

Dragons

Dragons

East wind

South wind

West wind

26 A high-scoring hand (48,757,784 points)

General Game Strategies

Elements of Sets

It is only in the exceptional case that you would actually be dealt complete sets. Typically, you must collect them in the course of the hand. While you are still new to Mah-Jongg, it is helpful to arrange your tiles according to the suits—balls, bamboos, and characters—as well as according to the honor tiles—winds and dragons. This way you can recognize where it might be possible to complete combinations, as the following examples show:

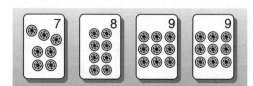

◆ Balls 7, 8, 9, 9   **27**
   Four possibilities present themselves: Either the sequence 7–8–9 or the pair 9–9. Suppose you receive a 6 to make the chow 6–7–8, and then, perhaps, another 9 for the pung 9.
◆ Bamboos 2, 2, 3   **28**
   Here, the chows 1–2–3 or 2–3–4 as well as the pung 2–2–2 could come about.
◆ Bamboos 2, 3, 6, 7   **29**
   The possible chows are: 1–2–3 or 2–3–4, as well as 5–6–7 or 6–7–8. Also, since you have so many bamboos, it is likely the other players will discard theirs.

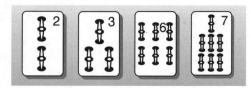

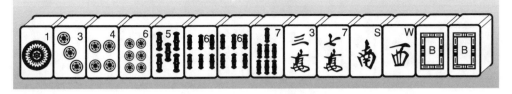

31 East's dealt tiles

32 South's dealt tiles

You could form a chow with bamboo tiles 1, 4, 5, or 8. Or you could make an end pair with a second 2, 3, 6, or 7.

◆ Characters 3, 4, 4, 6
With these elements. you have **30** makings of a pung from the existing 4–4 pair, or you could form the chows 2–3–4, 3–4–5, or 4–5–6.

Examples of Playing a Hand

Follow through these examples for the mixed-hand game to better understand the collecting of tiles and creating of sets. All take place in an East wind round. Each wind's drawn tiles are already arranged for easy reference according to suits and honor tiles (winds and dragons).

First Example

◆ East has: balls 1, 3, 4, 6; bamboos 5, 6, 6, 7; characters 3, 7; S, W, winds; two white dragons. **31**
◆ Balls: The chows 1–2–3, 2–3–4, 3–4–5, or 4–5–6 are possible.
◆ Bamboos: The chow 5, 6, 7 exists as well as the pair 6–6, which might make a pung.
◆ Characters: There are no elements here that look promising for collecting any sets. So East should discard one of the characters as his first discard.
◆ Winds: There are no elements that might promise a pung, but a wind end pair might come about.
◆ Dragons: The white dragon pair is worth 2 points, and maybe it could become a pung.

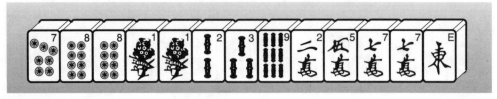

33 West's dealt tiles

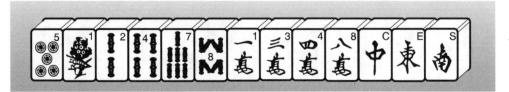

34 North's dealt tiles

◆ South has: balls 6, 9, 9; bamboos 5, 7; characters 1, 2, 5, 6; N, N, W, winds; a white dragon. **32**

◆ Balls: The existing pair 9–9 could be made into a pung.

◆ Bamboos: Tile 6 would make a chow.

◆ Characters: Tiles 3, 4, or 7 would complete a chow, or a matching tile might make an end pair.

◆ Winds: The north wind pair could become a pung.

◆ Dragons: The lone dragon will likely become a discard at some point.

◆ West has: balls 7, 8, 8; bamboos 1, 1, 2, 3, 9; characters 2, 5, 7, 7; E wind. **33**

◆ Balls: The chow 7–8–9 or the pung 8–8–8 could come about.

◆ Bamboos: West already has the chow 1–2–3 and the pair 1–1, which could become a pung.

◆ Characters: The exisitng pair 7–7 could be made into a pung.

◆ Winds: Since the lone wind tile is a round wind, West hopes to make a pair rather than discard it.

◆ North has: ball 5; bamboos 1, 2, 4, 7, 8; characters 1, 2, 4, 8; a red dragon; E, S winds. **34**

◆ Balls: North will discard this single tile.

◆ Bamboos: Chows 1–2–3, 2–3–4, 6–7–8, or 7–8–9 might come about.

◆ Characters: Chows 1–2–3, 2–3–4 or 3–4–5 could come about.

◆ Winds: North also hopes to draw a second East wind to make an end pair.

◆ Dragons: Depending on how the hand goes, North will discard this dragon or hope to make an end pair.

The Course of the Hand

Since East starts with 14 tiles, he is not allowed to draw one, but rather must initiate play by discarding one. He decides on character 7.

The next turn would have been South's, but West calls "pung," and melds his two character 7s with the claimed character 7 placed horizontally between them. Then West discards character 5.

The playing sequence now proceeds to the right with North! North calls "chow," melds the character chow 3–4–5, and discards ball 5. Remember that only the player to the right of the discard can claim that discard for a chow.

East calls "chow," melds the ball chow 4–5–6, and discards character 3.

South now, for the first time in the hand, engages in play, by declaring a chow. South melds the character chow 1–2–3, and discards the ball 6.

West calls "chow," melds the ball chow 6–7–8, and discards ball 8.

North draws a red dragon from the wall. He now has a red dragon pair in his hand, which can serve as his required end pair. North then discards character 8.

East draws bamboo 4, which could lead to a possible chow. In order to keep all his chances open for making sets with his suits, East discards the south wind tile.

South draws bamboo 8. He does not want to destroy the elelments he is collecting in bamboos,; he discards the west wind.

West draws ball 2. Since he cannot use it, he immediately discards it

North draws bamboo 5, giving him a chance to make a chow. He discards character 1.

East draws bamboo 3, giving him a concealed chow. He discards the west wind. This play seems quite harmless to East, since shortly beforehand South also discarded a west wind. And since it was not claimed, that means there are only two other west wind tiles still in play.

South draws a north wind tile, giving him a concealed pung. He discards his single white dargon. This is a risky move, but South is counting on making an end pair with either character 5 or 6.

East calls "pung," melds the white dragon pung, and discards bamboo 7.

It is South's turn again. He draws ball 2 and immediately discards it.

East calls "Mah-Jongg," claiming the ball 2 as his end tile. He does not have to discard a tile.

Settlement   35

East reveals all his sets and sorts out those that do not score any points. The scoreless sets are the ball chow 4–5–6, the bamboo chow 3–4–5, and the bamboo end pair 6–6.

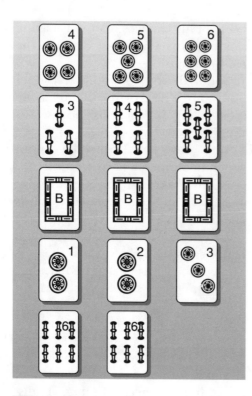

35 East's hand

Calculation	
Exposed dragon pung	4 points
Premium for last tile =	
center tile of the chow	2 points
Mah-Jongg (going out)	20 points
	26 points

Since the dragon pung brings a doubling of the overall points, East reaches 52 points. As dealer, he doubles that again and thus scores 104, receiving 100 (rounded) from each player; 300 points in total.

After South has sorted out his tiles that have no score, his concealed wind pung remains. It brings 8 points, which are in addition doubled once. That means, South has reached 16 points (20 rounded), which have to be settled with West and North.

West only has an exposed character pung 7—a 2 point total (0 rounded).

North must sort out all his tiles except for his dragon pair, which brings 2 points (0 rounded). South receives 20 points from West and North each. Since West and North have no points when rounded, their net result is 0 points.

Second Example

Here is a general outline of the dealt tiles and possible elements that each player can use to begin his collection. You should take the time to make a more precise analysis of the dealt tiles on your own.

◆ East has: balls 3, 4, 4, 6; bamboos 7, 8, 9, 9; characters 2, 2, 3, 5; a white dragon; E wind. **36**
East has chances in all suits to form chows and/or to make two pungs. In addition, there is the prospect for a valuable end pair with the honor tiles.

◆ South has: balls 9, 9, 9; bamboos 3, 4, 7, 8; characters 6, 8, 8; S, W winds; a green dragon **37**
South has a very good chance at a kong, a pung, a chow, and a pair with the honor tiles.

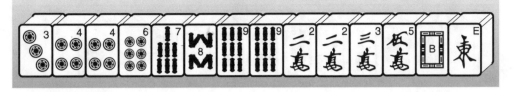

36 East's dealt tiles

37 South's dealt tiles

◆ West has: balls 1, 2, 8; bamboos 2, 4, 5, 6, 6, 6, 6; character 4; N, S, E winds. **38**

There are chances for chows and for a kong; also one prevailing wind tile gives hope for a valuable end pair.

◆ North has: balls 2, 3, 6, 7; bamboos 1, 1; characters 6, 6, 6; W wind; two red and one white dragon. **39**

North's dealt tiles are also good. He has chances for a kong, two more pungs, and one chow.

The Course of the Hand

East discards the white dragon. Even though that is a valuable honor tile, it does not make sense to destroy the good beginning elements in suits or to discard one's own wind tile.

South draws a south wind, now has a pair, and discards the west wind. His suit collection is too promising to keep the west wind tile.

West draws bamboo 6 and now has a concealed pung. He decides to keep this concealed, waiting to declare the pung at some later time. He discards character 4.

North draws character 4 from the wall and discards it immediately. It does not make any sense for him to destroy the existing pung—it could become a kong—in order to build a scoreless chow.

East declares "chow," lays out the character sequence 3–4–5, and discards ball 6.

South draws a green dragon and now has a pair. He immediately discards the character 6.

North calls "kong," melds the four immediately, draws from the dead wall character 1 as a supplement tile, and discards the white dragon.

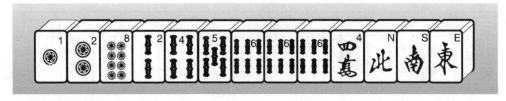

38 West's beginning tiles

39 North's beginning tiles

South draws a south wind again, and now has a concealed pung. He discards bamboo 4.

West draws a west wind. With some luck, he could make Mah-Jongg in four moves, but an opponent may go out sooner. Making a kong brings the most points, so he now declares the concealed kong, draws a tile from the dead wall, and discards the east wind.

North draws bamboo 1, making a concealed pung, and discards the west wind, since one is already dead.

East draws ball 8 and discards it.

South draws season tile 4 (north) and declares it. He draws bamboo 9 as a supplement tile. He now has a concealed chow, and discards bamboo 3.

West foregoes the chow call, since it does not bring any points. He hopes for something better from the wall, but draws a white dragon, which he immediately discards.

North draws ball 4, declares "chow," and discards ball 6.

East draws an east wind, making a pair, and he discards bamboo 9.

South draws character 8, adds it to make a concealed pung, and declares "Mah-Jongg."

Calculation	
Mah-Jongg (going out)	20 points
Concealed hand Mah-Jongg	20 points
Season tile	4 points
Concealed chow of terminal ball 9	8 points
Concealed pung of character 8	4 points
Concealed pung of S wind	8 points
Concealed dragon pair	2 points
Dragon end pair	2 points
Last tile, self-drawn	2 points
	70 points

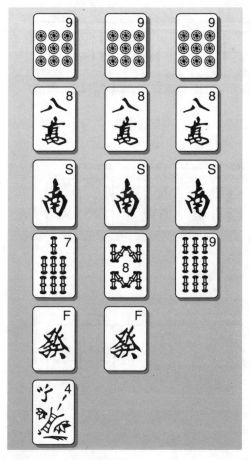

40 South's hand

Settlement

40

Having called "Mah-Jongg," South begins the process by sorting out the scoreless bamboo chow. He scores his hand at 70 points (see calculation on left page), and looks for doubles.

South's own wind pung brings a double two times; his final score is 280 points. West and North each pay this amount. East, as dealer, must pay double. South wins 1120 points total.

West gets 16 points (20 rounded) for his declared, concealed bamboo 6 kong. North gets 8 points for the exposed character 6 kong and 2 points for the dragon pair: 10 points overall. East own wind pair gets 2 points (0 rounded).

West gets paid 10 points (20–10 = 10) from North and 40 points (20 x 2 = 40) from East. North gets 20 points (10 x 2 = 20) from East. Since East has lost, the deal now moves to the right. South becomes "temporary" East.

Third Example

◆ East has: balls 4, 5, 7; bamboos 2, 4; characters 1, 3, 4, 8, 8; three red dragons; S wind. **41**

East has good elements in all suits for chows, as well as the prospect for a character pung and for a dragon kong.

◆ South has: balls 3, 4, 6, 9; bamboos 1, 3, 4, 6; characters 6, 6, 8; a green dragon; N wind. **42**

South has the chance to make chows in all suits, as well as a character pung.

◆ West has: balls 2, 3, 9; bamboos 5, 9; characters 4, 7, 7, 9; white and green dragons; two E winds. **43**

West has elements for ball and character chows, and for a pung of characters. The wind tiles are a prevailing wind pair that could be made into a pung.

◆ North has: balls 7, 8; bamboos 1, 2, 4, 7; characters 2, 2, 2; two white dragons; E, N winds **44**

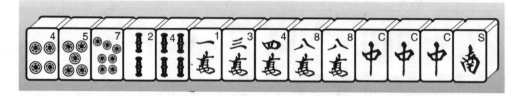

41 East's dealt tiles

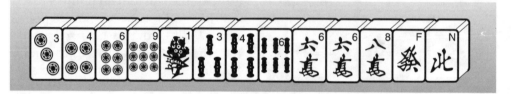

42 South's dealt tiles

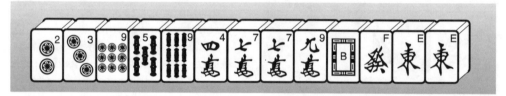

43 West's dealt tiles

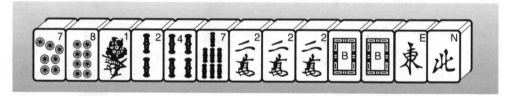

44 North's dealt tiles

North has good elements for making a ball or bamboo chow. The pung has a good chance of being expanded to make a kong. Similarly, the pair is a good prospect for expanding to make a pung.

The Course of the Hand

East discards the south wind.

South draws ball 3 and thus has a pair. Since he does not want to destroy his promising suit elements, he discards the dragon.

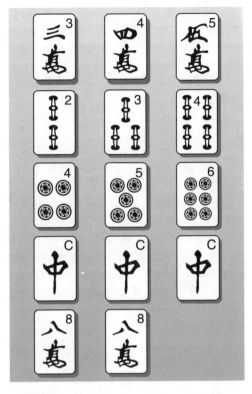

45 East's hand

North draws ball 6, completing a chow, and discards the east wind.

West calls "pung," melds the triple, and discards bamboo 5.

North draws bamboo 3, making a second concealed chow, and discards circle 7.

South calls "chow," melds his sequence, and discards the north wind.

West draws ball 4, making a concealed chow, and discards ball 9.

North draws bamboo 3, making a concealed chow, and he discards the north wind.

East draws ball 6, making his third concealed chow, and he declares a concealed hand Mah-Jongg. **45**

Settlement

Now you should make the settlement for all the players with the help of the tables. The answers are on page 47.

Fourth Example

You will see, in the middle of a hand, how a player tries to achieve a draw.

The Remaining Wall

There are only eight tiles left in the wall that can be drawn, and 14 in the dead wall: a total wall of 22 tiles.

A Reminder
When the entire wall has been exhausted without someone having made Mah-Jongg, the hand ends in a draw.

West draws character 7, making a concealed pung, and discards bamboo 9.

North draws character 2 and keeps the just-created kong concealed. He discards bamboo 7.

East draws character 5, making a concealed chow, and discards character 1.

South draws ball 5, making a concealed chow, and discards ball 9.

West draws a white dragon, and thus makes the requisite pair. He discards the green dragon.

Mid-Hand Distribution of Tiles

East has exposed a bamboo 3, 4, 5 chow, a character 7 pung, and a north wind pung. He holds in his hand balls 5 and 6 as well as two red dragons.

South has exposed a green dragon pung and a south wind pung. He holds in his hand bamboos 4, 5, 5 and characters 1, 2, 4, 4.

West has not yet melded anything and holds balls 2, 2, 4, 4, 6, 7, bamboo 8, a west wind pair, a white dragon pair, and a red dragon pair.

North has exposed a ball 7–8–9 chow, a bamboo 9 pung, and an east wind pung. He holds in his hand balls 4, 6, character 8 and a white dragon pair.

West considers the following:

◆ There are only eight wall tiles left that can be drawn.
◆ He will lose the game with his two concealed pairs (4 points).
◆ The opponents presumably have elements of sets in their hands, with which they might make Mah-Jongg.

West decides that his best strategy is to force a draw by discarding only tiles that he is fairly sure none of his opponents can use.

The Course of the Hand

West draws bamboo 3 and keeps it. Even though it does not go with what he has in his hand, it could be used by someone else. Since in the course of the hand, once before, a west wind tile

was discarded, he destroys his west wind pair to make a discard that, presumably, no one can take, except by declaring Mah-Jongg.

North draws ball 6 and discards character 8.

East draws bamboo 2 and immediately discards it.

South draws character 4, making a concealed pung, and discards bamboo 4.

West draws ball 5 and discards his second west wind tile.

With this discard it should be clear to the other players, if they are paying attention, what West's strategy is.

North draws a green dragon and discards it. That, however, is a strategic mistake:

◆ South has already laid out a green dragon pung, and cannot claim North's discard to declare a kong; South can only make a kong by drawing. Nobody else can use the tile either.
◆ If North had seen through West's strategy, he would have tried to help another player make Mah-Jongg, rather than letting the game end in a draw, with no score for anyone.

North then would have gotten points, at least from West, whose tactics signal a very bad hand.
◆ By discarding the green dragon, North will probably not get any points at all, unless another player draws a wall tile with which he can make Mah-Jongg.

East, however, has been able to see through West's tactics:

◆ East draws character 2. Even though it does not go with his tiles, he keeps it.

He lays down a red dragon, which maybe someone else can claim.

◆ West holds the red dragon pair, but he does not want to call "pung," because there is only one more tile that can be drawn from the wall, and he hopes that South cannot use this tile to make Mah-Jongg.

South draws character 6 and discards it again. The hand ends in a draw. The deal passes to the right, and a new hand begins.

Fourth Quiz

1 Which player determines the value of his hand first at the end of the hand?

A East

B The Mah-Jongg caller

C The player who sits to the left of the Mah-Jongg caller

2 Which player gets double the number of points from all the others when he wins the hand?

3 How many points does a player get for:

A His own wind pair?

B A flower or season tile of his own wind? of another player's wind?

C A declared, concealed dragon kong?

D Declaring Mah-Jongg?

4 How often does the number of points get doubled for:

A A pung made of dragons?

B A pung made of one's own wind?

C A kong made of winds? of prevailing winds?

D A flower or season tile of one's own wind direction?

5 Calculate, on the basis of the picture, how many points East receives from each opponent after he has made Mah-Jongg in the East wind round. **46**

6 When must a supplement tile be drawn for a kong?

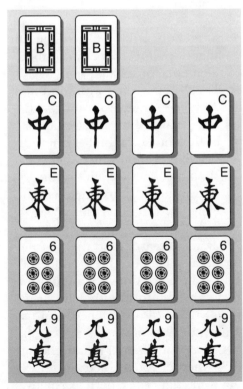

46 East's hand

Answers: page 47

Personal Strategy

Advice on your personal strategy cannot, of course, be put to use right away, or in each single hand. Read through these suggestions and begin to absorb them, and you will increase your enjoyment as well as your success when playing traditional and mixed-hand Mah-Jongg.

Keep in Mind
Three things are essential for each hand: attentive observation—who melds and discards which tiles; quick reactions; and, based on these, a flexible strategy that can be varied as the hand progresses.

The Beginning of the Hand and the First Moves

As soon as you have set up your dealt tiles—in your rack or standing on the table—make a definite plan of which sets you want to collect. At first, you should aim for a high point score.

Keep your strategy flexible, so that you can consider other sets as they become possible, and so that you are not dependent on getting only one tile.

Plan your hand in such a way that you might later on have several possible ways to declare Mah-Jongg—chows are the easiest sets to complete, but they score no points. If you have been dealt—besides dragon and wind tiles—several tiles of all three suits, then you should not decide to collect only one suit:

◆ At first discard the tiles of the suit that does not show any sensible elements for making sets.
◆ Then do the same with wind tiles (but keep your own wind), and after that with the dragon tiles.
◆ In the course of the hand it will become evident which tiles you should collect (based on your drawn tiles, discards made or claimed, and other calls made).

Always discard first the so-called terminal tiles, i.e., the 1 and 9 of a suit—which are not very useful, since they can only form either the beginning or end of a sequence, and thus limit your flexibility.

Before you claim a tile, think carefully whether you are actually improving your chances or, perhaps, inadvertently giving away your strategy.

In the beginning play of the hand, you should discard wind tiles that are not your own wind, since at that early stage it is quite unlikely that the other players would be able to use them to declare pung or kong.

When you realize early in the hand that a player seems to be collecting certain wind or dragon tiles, then discard them as soon as possible, so that they may become dead tiles and an opponent will not be able to use them in the decisive end phase to make Mah-Jongg.

Always play against the player who appears strongest (the one with the highest score), and try to defeat his strategy.

The better you know all the point scores, premiums, and doublings for sets by heart, the easier you can use them to figure your chances.

Even though each player should have the tables next to him for reference, you will be too distracted, destroy the rhythm of play, and upset the other players if you have to stop and leaf through the pages of tables in a lengthy search.

The Further Course of the Hand

As the hand progresses, it becomes increasingly important to stick to a plan, once it has been made, and not to let yourself be overly impressed by a drawn tile with a high value that does not otherwise fit into your hand. It is easy to be tempted, for example, to speculate on making a high-scoring pair or pung, and so discard in turn tiles of less point value which have a much greater possibility for making critical sets.

As long as possible, keep the other players in the dark about your collection strategy. However, try to see through the tactics of your opponents as quickly as possible. Based on your observations, strengthen your own hand by discarding the tiles that your opponents do not collect.

Keep dragon tiles in your hand as long as possible. Every player strives to hold on to these honor tiles, because they do not destroy a suit hand (see the chapter on "Special Hands," starting on page 48), and they are valuable.

If you have had a great deal of luck in the deal and in the early drawing of tiles, so that you have a hand with high points and possibilities for doublings, then you should continue to develop it and not destroy the hand by being tempted to make easy, but worthless, sets—even if you run the risk that an opponent may make Mah-Jongg.

A Reminder
A hand that is incomplete is continually being evaluated. Remember that high-scoring sets are worthwhile, but sometimes a quick, low-scoring hand is the best way to win consistently!

The Last Moves and the End of the Hand

You can recognize that a hand is in the last stages, and may be ending soon, when it is clear that the other players have melded a lot and there are so few tiles in the wall that you might be able to draw only two or three times more at the most.

Towards the end of the hand, you should discard any tiles that have already been discarded twice or three times or that have been melded in sets. It is unlikely that a pung or even the end-pair for Mah-Jongg could be declared with them.

When you think that your hand is hopeless—that there is little chance that you will score many points—you should try to force a draw to end the hand.

Discard those tiles that the other players in all probability will not be able to claim. To block the other players in this way, you will have to, under certain circumstances, destroy your concealed sets that you have worked to complete.

If you want to avoid a draw, strive to end the hand by making chows, because they are the easiest sets to complete.

If you have a number of high-value sets, but cannot find a way to end the hand, then help an opponent—if possible the player who seems weakest — to make Mah-Jongg. That is the only chance you may have to benefit from your high-value hand.

The points that you must pay out to the Mah-Jongg caller, in such a case, are most likely to be relatively low in comparison to the points that you will receive from the two other players.

Discard an honor tile only when the same tile has already been discarded. If none has, you must assume that one or several opponents have them in their hands and can claim it.

Penalties

Only when all four players have sufficiently mastered the game, should penalties for certain wrong behaviors be imposed. Only when the play is severely hampered or other players are greatly disadvantaged should penalties be enforced for such things as gross inattention or negligence.

The agreed-on penalty points have to be paid out to all co-players. In this case also, East receives double the number of points or must pay double the number of points.

When a player, for whatever reason, has too many or too few tiles, he is declared "dead." Even though he must continue to play, his game is not counted in the settlement. He must, however, pay out the full number of points to each player. Here also, East receives or pays double.

When a player mistakenly declares "Mah-Jongg," but realizes his mistake before any of the other players have displayed their hands, then play may continue:

- The mistaken Mah-jongg caller must pick up his tiles again, as a penalty. Thus, his collection strategy is known to his opponents.
- If any of the other players have already displayed their hands, the hand ends.
- If play is ended, the mistaken Mah-Jongg caller's hand is considered worthless.
- The mistaken Mah-Jongg caller must pay the number of points reached by everyone else. Here also, East receives or pays double.
- When one player draws another player's attention to a mistake and that player can correct the mistake, then the one who has discovered the mistake can be made to pay punishment points. This is because the other two players have been disadvantaged through the correction.

The player who has mistakenly declared Mah-Jongg gets zero points at the end—even if he has not exposed his hand, or if he is later able to go out succesfully with a different arrangement.

As long as the next move (the player to the right drawing a tile from the wall or any player claiming the discarded tile) has not been made, a player can correct an error with no penalty.

Incorrect scoring or payment may be punished.

A wrong announcement of the discarded tile may be punished.

Many of these and other penalties are not used in informal play. However, the penalty most often imposed is a point penalty for incorrectly declaring "chow," "pung," or "kong." Typically a 100-point penalty is imposed, to go to the eventual winner of the game (after four rounds).

Answers to the Quizzes

First Quiz page 13

1. 144 tiles
2. 36 tiles
3. 52 tiles
4. Flowers and seasons
5. West
6. Suit tiles: balls, bamboos, characters
   Honor tiles: winds and dragons

Second Quiz page 16

1. The correct answer is A; C is contained in this answer.
2. East (dealer), South, West, North.
3. To the right of the wall break is the the dead wall.
   The tiles are distributed from the left of the wall break.
4. East gets 14 tiles; all the other players get 13.

Third Quiz page 19

1. B and C are correct; A is wrong, because all tiles inside the walls, except for the last one discarded, are "dead."
2. The tiles lie face up inside the walls, but not in the middle. Each player must lay down his tiles just inside the wall in front of him.
3. One discards one tile for each tile that is taken.
4. B is correct.
5. By claiming the last discarded tile before the player whose turn it is has taken a tile.
6. With "chow" one completes a sequence, with "pung" a triplet, with "kong" four of a kind.
7. C is correct.

Fourth Quiz page 41

1. B is correct.
2. East
3.
   A. 2 points
   B. 4 points each
   C. 32 points
   D. 20 points

4

A 1 x

B 2 x

C of winds: 2 x,
of prevailing winds: 3 x

D 1 x

5 Mah-Jongg (going out) 20 points
Exposed kongs of dragons, winds
and nines: 3 x 16   = 48 points
Exposed kong of sixes = 8 points
Dragon end pair   = 2 points

_____

                       78 points

4 kongs	= double 4 x
Wind kong	= double 2 x
Dragon kong	= double 2 x
Prevailing wind kong	= double 3 x
Own wind kong	= double 3 x

_____

                   double 14 x
              = 1,277,952 points
              = 1,277,950 (rounded)

East gets paid double this number
of points from each player
(2,555,900).

6 When you complete the kong
with a self-drawn tile from the
wall, at the time you choose to
declare and meld it you must
then draw a supplement tile. In
addition, when you form a kong
from a melded pung, you must
draw a supplement tile.

Settlement for the Third Example
page 39

After East has sorted out the scoreless
pair and chows, he scores his points as
follows:

Mah-Jongg (going out)	20 points
Concealed hand Mah-Jongg	20 points
Concealed dragon pung	8 points
Last tile, self-drawn	2 points

_____

                         50 points

The dragon pung brings a simple
doubling, i.e., 100 points, and South,
West, and North must pay double that
amount: 200 points each to East.

South has 0 points.

West calculates:

Concealed dragon pair	2 points
Exposed wind pung	4 points
Concealed pung of character 7	4 points

_____

                         10 points

West's own wind pung brings a double
two times; his final score is 40 points.

North gets 2 points for his dragon
pair and 4 points for his concealed
kong, i.e., 6 points, rounded to 10.

Settling between losers, South pays
West 40 points, North pays West 30,
and South pays North 10 points.

Special Hands

When you have mastered the standard mixed-hand game of traditional Mah-Jongg, you and your group can come to an agreement to take up **special hands**. Before the beginning of the first hand of a game, everyone should decide which hands are permissible in your group and which are not.

The special hands can be subdivided into four groups:

◆ Suit hands
◆ Honor hands
◆ Pair hands
◆ Extra hands

Special hands require a great deal of good fortune compared to the standard hands. Much depends on the luck of the deal, the draw, and the discards of your opponents.

These hands can be successful only when you:

◆ have the respective elements in your hand from the beginning of the dealt tiles.
◆ execute your game consistently.
◆ have practice and thus are equipped with skills and precise knowledge of the game.

The rules for special hands prescribe uniformity of suit, particular sequences, combinations of sets, and/or certain sets of rare honor tiles. Since it is so difficult to complete these hands successfully, they have a high value, and, except for the pure and the clean suit hands, they can even have a value related to the limit or a fixed point value between 1000 and 3000 points.

Basic Hands with Doublings

To these belong the suit hands, which fall into two categories:

◆ The pure suit hand, and
◆ The clean suit hand.

Pure Suit

Here, the combinations of the completed hand—chows, pungs, and kongs—consist of only one basic suit: either only of balls, only of bamboos, or only of characters. That means you have only 36 possible tiles available. If agreed upon, you can allow an exception, in which the end pair consists of wind or of dragon tiles, instead of the suit.

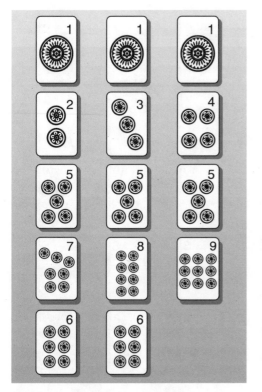

47 Pure ball suit hand; end pair: balls

48 Pure characters suit hand exception; end pair: red dragons

For the settlement, you determine the number of points for your sets as well as the premium points. Then you double the total amount:

◆ If the end pair consists of the basic suit, then you also double four times. 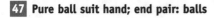**47**
◆ If the end pair consists of wind or dragon tiles, then you also double three times. **48**

Example

You dealt tiles are: balls 2, 2, 3, 4, 5, 7, 7, 8, 9, bamboo 3, two green dragons, and the north wind. It is obvious, that you already have with the balls alone good elements for chows and pungs, or even for kongs. Due to the green dragon pair, which can be planned as a possible end pair, you can dare to play a pure suit hand with a dragon end pair.

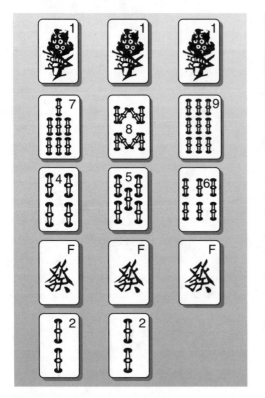

49 Clean suit hand with dragon combination

50 Clean suit hand with two wind combinations

The first tiles, which you should discard as useless, are the north wind and the bamboo 3.

If you draw another ball, then you can consider also discarding the dragon pair, should the opportunity come about, and concentrating on a pure suit hand. If you should draw, in the course of the hand, unsuitable tiles, you can switch to a standard Mah-Jongg hand. The strategy depends solely on your readiness to take on risk.

Clean Suit   **49** **50**

You again collect sets of one basic suit, but also of wind and/or dragon tiles. You are allowed to form maximally two sets of the honor tiles.

Since the clean suit hand is more easily achieved than the pure hand—you have 64 possible tiles available—it is less valuable.

When you have determined the total number of points, you double that amount:

- If the hand contains a dragon or a wind set, you double twice. **49**
- If the hand contains two dragon or wind sets, you double once. **50**

Advantages of the Suit Hands

In addition to the doublings, a suit hand offers the following advantages:

- The Mah-Jongg hand may consist of any number of chows. That is an essential relief.
- You can wait to decide between pure and clean suit hands.
- If a suit hand becomes hopeless, it can be changed at any time into a standard mixed hand.
- Only the player who makes Mah-Jongg with his suit hand gets paid. The other players do not settle their hands or exchange points.

Strategy for Suit Hands

Keep dragon and wind tiles in your hand as long as possible. This is so that you will to be able to use them to build either a pung—for a clean suit hand—or the end pair, even when the doublings will be less.

Discard first the suit which the player to your left seems to be collecting.

Try to play in such a way that you can switch from the suit hand to the standard mixed hand.

Hands with Set Point Values

With the standard mixed hand and the suit hand, the final point score achieved depends on how you have formed your sets.

In the following, you will become familiar with many special Mah-Jongg hands, whose scoring is assigned a fixed point value right from the start. The individual combinations are not scored separately. The hand receives an automatic point score.

The point values indicated for the following hands are guidelines; your group may agree on other scorings, such as multiples of a set limit.

Nine Lanterns (Heavenly Gates)— 3000 Points   **51**

The nine lanterns, also called by other names, including the "heavenly gates," resembles the pure suit hand, because it consists of only one suit. You must make these sets:

- One pung (or kong), each made of terminals, i.e., with the numbers 1 and 9,
- One sequence of seven simples, numbers 2 through 8,
- Any suit of your choosing.

It is worthwhile for you to choose a nine lantern hand, instead of a suit hand, when you have been dealt some tiles of the numbers 1 and 9 of the same suit as well as part of the sequence 2 through 8.

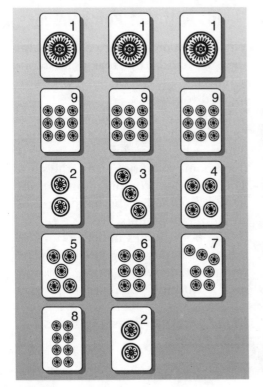

51 Nine lantern hand (heavenly gates)

52 Pure four friends hand (four blessings)

The following hands are called "honor hands," because they make use of the honor tiles (the dragons and winds) in special ways.

Four Friends Hands

These hands are also called the "four blessings." They can be completed successfully only by making a pung with each of the four winds as:

◆ The pure four friends hand or
◆ The clean four friends hand.

Pure Four Friends— 3000 Points

52

For any chances of success, you must be dealt three or four wind pairs, and since you can build your pungs from only 16 tiles, you need a lot of luck.

As soon as your opponents realize that you have a four friends hand in mind, they will try to prevent it. They will keep their wind tiles concealed in their hands and would rather destroy collected sets, even if the hand ends in a draw.

53 Clean four friends hand

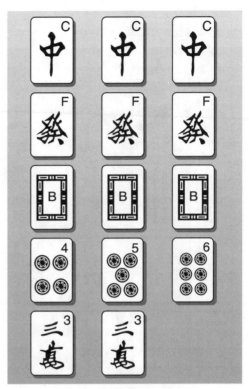

54 Three great scholars

A four friends hand that has become hopeless can be changed into a clean suit hand, since wind tiles are allowed. The advantage is that your opponents do not know which suit you are now collecting.

Clean Four Friends— 2000 Points

53

A simplification is the clean four friends game, for which you collect not only wind, but also dragon pungs. You have 28 tiles to choose from.

Three Great Scholars —2000 Points

54

Here, it is not a matter of certain suit or honor tiles, but rather of specific prescribed sets:

◆ Three dragon pungs and/or kongs,
◆ Any kind of a chow, pung, or kong, and
◆ Any end pair.

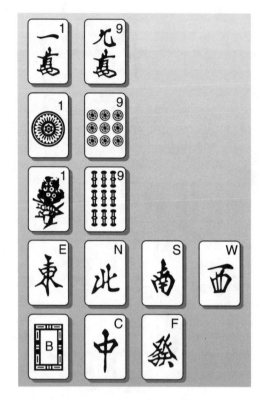

55 **Unpaired hand (unique wonders or thirteen impossible)**

The following hands are called the "pair hands." A kong is considered to be two pairs.

Unpaired (Unique Wonders)— 3000 Points   `55`

This is the only Mah-Jongg hand that is won with 13 tiles—also called the Thirteen Impossible.

The sets, which have to be formed, are fixed:

◆ One of each number 1 and 9 in each suit: balls 1, 9; bamboos 1, 9; and characters 1, 9.
◆ One of each wind: east, south, west, and north.
◆ One of each of the three dragons: white, red, and green.
    This hand is only possible when you have been dealt five or six of the required tiles.

Twins of the Earth— 2000 Points   `56`

This hand is also known as the "dirty pairs." You must form overall seven pairs of any kind:

◆ Any suit pairs (tiles 1 to 9),
◆ Any dragon and/or wind pairs.

Twins of the Sky (Honor Pairs)— 3000 Points   `57`

Here, you must put any seven pairs together as such:

◆ Terminal suit pairs: the numbers 1, 1 and/or 9, 9,
◆ Honor tiles pairs: dragons and/or winds.

Twins of Hell— 3000 Points

This game consists of seven pairs of the suits numbers 2 through 7. It must not contain any 1, 9, or honor tile pairs!

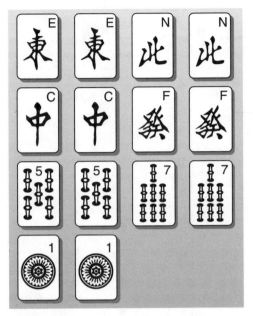

56 Twins of the earth (dirty pairs)

57 Twins of the sky (honor pairs)

Heavenly Twins—
4000 Points

This hand is made of seven pairs in the same suit.

Terminals—
2000 Points

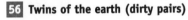
58

This is also called "heads and tails." The complete hand consists only of the tiles 1 and 9 in pungs or kongs, and you must form also the end pair with the terminal tiles of one suit.

The following hands are called extra hands. There are no overlapping categories.

All Honors—
2000 Points

◆ The hand is composed of four pungs and/or kongs, which must consist of the numbers 1 and/or 9, and dragons and/or winds.

◆ You must form the end pair with the numbers 1 or 9.

◆ The sets can be of any suit.

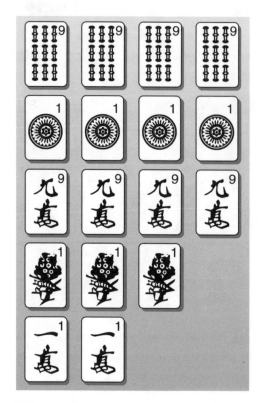

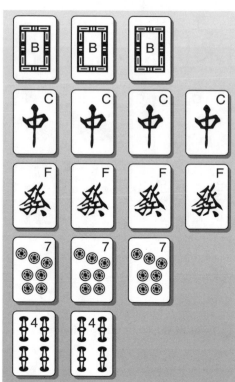

58 Terminal tile hand (heads and tails)

59 Dragon hand

Four Kongs—
3000 Points

◆ For this hand, you must collect four kongs of any kind and one end pair.

◆ You need overall 18 tiles: This number results from the supplement tiles, which you receive for each exposed and for each declared, concealed kong.

◆ If you are not already dealt pairs and one pung, the four kongs hand can hardly succeed.

Dragon—
2000 Points

59

For this, you must make three dragon pungs or kongs as well as a pung or kong of any kind, and an end pair of any kind.

Keep in Mind

You cannot convert a pung that you formed with a discard into a kong by claiming another discard. Only one discard is permitted in a kong!

Moon—1000 Points

For this, there are no prescribed sets, but the moon hand is defined in this way:

Bamboo 1 is drawn as the last tile from the wall to make Mah-Jongg or is claimed as the last discard.

Fruits—1000 Points

Also for this hand, there are no pre-scribed sets.

If you have bamboo 5 in your hand and make Mah-Jongg, then it is a fruits hand.

Heaven's Grace—1000 Points

Here we deal with the shortest hand possible, also called "the going out of the gods."

If immediately after the deal East has a complete hand (he has his original 14 tiles!), and he declares Mah-Jongg, then his call means that he has received "heaven's grace."

Earth's Grace—1000 Points

When South, West, or North, after the deal, has a complete hand, and can make Mah-Jongg with East's first discard or the first drawn tile, one speaks of "earth's grace."

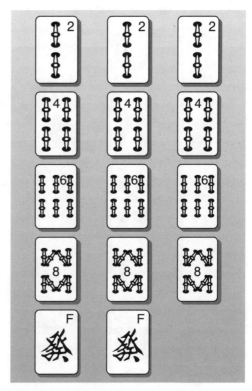

60 All green hand

All Green—3000 Points ⬛60

In traditional Chinese Maḥ-Jongg circles, besides the green dragons, the bamboo tiles 2, 3, 4, 6, and 8 are called green tiles.

You form a complete green hand with:

◆ Pungs and/or kongs of the respective bamboo or dragon tiles.
◆ A green end pair.

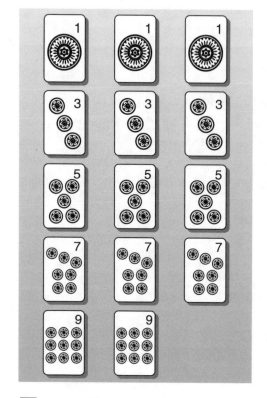

61 Winding snake

62 Sky ladder

Winding Snake— 3000 Points   **61**

A complete hand consists of four pungs of the same suit, which have the numbers 1, 3, 5, and 7 as well as the end pair 9 of the same suit or of a dragon or wind pair. This can be made a little easier for the player: instead of the pung 1, you may also form the pung 9 and, accordingly, instead of the end pair 9, the pair 1.

Sky Ladder— 3000 Points   **62**

This Mah-Jongg hand consists of four suit pungs.

The respective number for each pung must rise in a sequence from pung to pung.

The suits of the pungs are not prescribed.

The hand is completed with an end pair of any kind.

Three Pungs of the Same Kind—2000 Points

The hand consists of:

◆ One pung each in every suit with the same number (for example balls 3, bamboo 3, character 3).
◆ Any kind of pung or kong.
◆ Any kind of end pair.

Jump Chows—3000 Points

One forms:

◆ Four chows that do not have a straight number sequence, but rather skip a number, for example, 1–3–5 or 2–4–6 (jump chows).
◆ Any kind of end pair.

Great Chow—1000 Points

For this you need:

◆ Three chows of only one suit, 1–2–3, 4–5–6 and 7–8–9.
◆ Any kind of pung or kong.
◆ Any kind of end pair.

Suit Hands

Pure Suit	double 4 x
Pure Suit, end pair of honors	double 3 x
Clean Suit	
(contains one wind or dragon set)	double 2 x
Clean Suit	
(contains two wind or suit sets)	double 1 x
Nine Lantern	3000 points

Honor Hands

Pure Four Friends	3000 points
Clean Four Friends	3000 points
Three Great Scholars	2000 points

Pair Hands

Unpaired (Unique Wonders or Thirteen Impossible)	3000 points
Twins of the Earth (Paired)	2000 points
Twins of the Sky (Honor Pairs)	3000 points
Twins of Hell	3000 points
Heavenly Twins	4000 points
Terminal Tiles	2000 points

Extra Hands

All Honors	2000 points
Dragon	2000 points
Four Kongs	3000 points
Moon	1000 points
Fruits	1000 points
Heaven's Grace	1000 points
Earth's Grace	1000 points
All Green	3000 points
Winding Snake	3000 points
Sky Ladder	3000 points
Three Pungs of the Same Kind	2000 points
Jump Chows	3000 points
Great Chow	1000 points

Japanese Mah-Jongg

Traditional Chinese Mah-Jongg and Japanese Mah-Jongg use essentially the same rules. The greatest differences, which you need to keep in mind if you want to play the Japanese variation, are in the mixed-hand game.

Bonus Tiles

Since obtaining the flowers and seasons is a matter of chance—and even though they bring points, they have no real strategic importance to the game—they are not used. Japanese Mah-Jongg is therefore played with only 136 tiles.

Scoring

In contrast to the mixed-hand game, in the Japanese variation only the complete hand of the Mah-Jongg caller is counted and paid by the losers.

East, just as before, receives and pays double the number of points. The losing players do not score their points or settle with each other. The Japanese game has also adopted a rule that if a player goes out on a discarded tile, he must be paid only by the person who discarded the tile, and not by the other players. Thus a careless player brings disaster upon himself only. Many see advantages:

◆ The Mah-Jongg caller always wins the hand, since no other player can score points with an incomplete hand.

◆ Since all players are under great pressure to make Mah-Jongg first—rather than collect sets which score a lot of points—this kind of game is faster and more exciting than the mixed hand.

The strategic aspects are more intense and suspenseful, because you must consider several collection possibilities and be able to readjust defensively very quickly to form other sets. After all, you have only one goal, which is to go out, and end the game first—to win!

Betting

When a player has not yet melded tiles, but only needs one tile to make Mah-Jongg, he is allowed to declare his hand "ready," and make a bet that he will make Mah-Jongg first.

He places the tiles of his hand face down with a bone (usually 100 or 200 points) on top:

◆ If he wins his bet, then the value of his hand, which the opponents have to pay, doubles.
◆ If one of his opponents wins the hand, then that person receives the bone.

In Japanese Mah-Jongg, all of the players must agree on house rules and on how to score, just as with traditional Chinese or mixed-hand Mah-Jongg. How many points a bet costs is also agreed upon in advance.

Glossary

Bonus tiles The eight "luck tiles," flowers and seasons. They are not used in play to form sets, but rather they are declared and laid down face up immediately after they have been drawn in the mixed-hand game. They have scoring advantages. For each bonus tile, one takes a supplement tile from the dead wall. Bonus tiles are not used in the Japanese variation.

Call Declaration made to interrupt the order of play to one's favor by claiming the tile which was last discarded, with which a combination can be completed or with which a player can end the hand. The combinations must be laid out immediately after the call.

The calls are: "chow," "pung," "kong," and "Mah-Jongg" or "out."

Chow 1. Sequence. A set, which can be laid only with tiles of the same suit. It consists of three directly consecutive numbers.

2. The call. You can declare "chow" by claiming the last discard—only from your left—or drawing a tile and melding it to complete a sequence. A drawn-tile chow does not need to be declared, but can be kept concealed in your hand.

Combinations *See* Sets.

Dead wall The part which is to the right of the wall break, from which supplement tiles are drawn.

Dead tiles The tiles which are discarded inside the wall and not immediately claimed. They can no longer be used in play.

Four *See* Kong

Honor tiles The white, red, and green dragons and the four winds (East, South, West, North). There are four of each (28 honor tiles).

Kong 1. A set of four tiles of the same kind.

2. The call. You can declare "kong" by claiming the last discard or by drawing a tile. The declared kong must be melded. It is said to be exposed if it includes a discard—and it can only include one discard. When the kong is melded, a supplement tile must be drawn from the dead wall. A drawn-tile, concealed kong does not need to be declared, but can be kept in your hand.

Loose tiles The seventh stack, which forms the wall break. The top tile is placed onto the third, the lower one onto the fifth tile of the dead wall.

Mah-Jongg 1. With the Mah-Jongg call, the hand is ended.

2. The call., You can declare "Mah-Jongg" or "out" in order to end the hand with the last discarded tile or a drawn tile.

Own wind For each player, the wind of the same name as his position. A player who has a set of his own wind direction has scoring advantages.

Pair Two tiles of the same kind; obligatory for a complete hand.

Prevailing winds Each round (at least four hands) is named for a wind, and this wind is said to "prevail" during that round. A set of the prevailing wind has scoring advantages.

Pung 1. A triplet. A set which consists of three tiles of the same kind.

2. The call. You can declare "pung" by claiming the last discard or by drawing a tile. The declared pung must be melded. It is said to be exposed if it includes a discard. A drawn-tile, concealed pung does not need to be declared, but can be kept in your hand. A concealed pung that is declared is said to be a declared, concealed pung.

Robbery of the kong Two players call at the same time "kong" and "Mah-Jongg." The Mah-Jongg call is higher, and that player receives the tile. This is referred to as ending the hand by "robbery of the kong."

Round There are four rounds to a game. A round is complete when all four players have held and lost the deal. If the dealer wins the hand, he deals again. There are at least four hands per round, but there is no limit to the number of dealer's extra hands.

Round winds Each round is played with a prevailing wind. A game begins with the East round, and the East wind prevails, then follow South, West, and North rounds. Prevailing wind tiles have scoring advantages. Any player whose own wind is also the prevailing wind is said to have "double wind."

Sequence *See* Chow

Sets Certain combinations collected in order to achieve a complete hand: a pair, sequence (chow), triplet (pung), or set of four (kong).

Stack Two tiles, one on top of the other, in the wall.

Supplement tile Anyone who receives flower or season tiles or who melds a kong, draws a supplement tile from the dead wall.

Suit tiles Tiles numbered 1 through 9 in three suits: balls, bamboos, and characters. There are four sets of each number (108 suit tiles).

Triplet *See* Pung

Wall break The procedure by which the wall is broken to locate where East starts the deal.

Wall The arrangement of tiles, for dealing and during play, in rows of stacks around the table.

Winds 1. The four winds: East, South, West, and North.

2. *See also* Own wind, Prevailing winds, *and* Round winds

Index